Celeb

Seeing Jesus in the
Festivals of the Jews

Table of Contents

Dedication

This book is dedicated to the Chula Vista church of Christ. At the time I was writing this book, we had been slowly, and sometimes painfully, going through the gospels. In them, we have been taking critical looks at how the writers used the Law, Prophets and Psalms to identify who Jesus is, what His teachings meant (and mean) and what His actions represent. As our guide, we have been using *Reading Backwards* by Richard Hays. This book is based on a series of lectures professor Hays gave at the Hulsean Lectures in the Faculty of Divinity at Cambridge University. As one might imagine, as I prepared for the classes, I often found myself swimming in waters deeper than I ever had before. It may be safe to say that all of us who participated in this class were "out of our league".

However, I prefer to swim in the deep, unchartered waters than to stay in the comfort of the known streams I typically wade in. It is in these deeper waters that we find ourselves growing, stretching and becoming more like the Christ we serve and follow.

I want to thank the members who have faithfully come to every Bible class and endured the often technical and complex studies we have done. I am grateful for your presence and participation. May this book be a blessing to all who read it.

Introduction

Before reading this book, it will be helpful to understand a couple of preliminary points.

First, it should be noted that I am writing this book as I feel that the books of the Old Testament have been largely overlooked or ignored. The first two chapters are dedicated purely to the task of generating a desire to go back to the older scriptures, just as Jesus did and calls us to do.

Certainly we know many of the events from the Old Testament, perhaps even from childhood, but outside of some very good stories of plagues, slings, floods and furnaces, it seems that we do not look to these passages of scripture as a means of better understanding our God and His Son, Jesus the Messiah. How do these stories fit into the story of God becoming flesh? How do they fit into the overall narrative that God is telling?

Typically, to gain better understandings of Jesus and who He was and is, we go straight to the Gospels, or even to the New Testament epistles, but rarely do we go to Leviticus or Nehemiah. Why would we? They don't even mention Him!

I believe that when we fail to go back to the ancient texts of the Jews, we do it to our own spiritual impoverishment. As we shall see in the first chapter, Jesus Himself calls us to search the Jewish scriptures to better understand Him and the Father who sent Him.

While Jesus certainly does call His followers to look at the Old Testament to see Him, this book will focus on the Jewish festivals that were mandated in the Law of Moses and celebrated throughout time. As we will see, understanding the purpose of the feasts, festivals and appointed times, how they were celebrated and what they symbolized, will give us a much clearer understanding as to the teachings and actions of Jesus. We may find that when we are done with this study, many of the teachings we thought we knew are quite different than we had supposed. If, in fact, our initial understandings are not completely off base, we will truly be adding layers of depth and power to the passages that we have read and loved for so long.

I hope and pray that as you read, you are falling more in love with Jesus, God's word and His promises that are acted out in the deeply ritualistic[1] and meaning-laden celebrations of the Jews.

---

[1] Though many may see this word as a negative, there is nothing wrong with rituals. They can and should be a good thing.

Part One

The Call to See Jesus in the Old Testament

Chapter One

Open Our Eyes

Then their eyes were opened….and they

knew Him

Luke 24:31

It was the loneliest road ever walked. Dirty and winding, the road seemed to stretch on endlessly. It was, perhaps, the longest seven-mile journey any human has ever attempted to make. Two people were leaving Jerusalem with heads hung low and tensions wired high.

This Passover weekend should have been joyous and hope-filled. They went to celebrate the power of their mighty God who saves, rescues and redeems. The God who sends plagues and frees the captives. The God who oppresses the oppressor and vindicates His people. He parts the sea and destroys the enemy, but the one they believed God had sent to bring Israel back from the death of captivity and cruel oppression of the Romans had Himself been put to death. They killed Him on a cross, like any criminal or would-be leader who dared to rival Caesar or simply cause too much trouble. Nails in His hands and His feet. His flesh torn from His body. His heart pierced with a spear. These two lonely travelers imagined their dreams, hopes and aspirations were now rotting in a tomb. Cleopas and his companion find themselves angry, hurt and confused. "One foot in front of the other" they must have thought; "just keep moving." Will this journey ever end?

Our two travelers begin to argue with one another as they go to the now lost town known as Emmaus. Despite their best efforts, they are unable to come to terms with what has happened. Nothing seemed to be as it should have been. Just before they left Jerusalem, forced to spend the weekend there because of the Sabbath regulations, they heard reports from their friends that certain women who followed Jesus with them had seen angels in a vision. The angels told them that their dead leader had risen. But this can't be true. Dreams and visions formed in the depths of sorrow shouldn't be trusted; it is best to leave.

As they travel down the road, hurting and lost, a stranger overhears their conversation and joins them on the road. Here He meets them on the path; where He emerged from is unknown. But there He is, and He has decided to make their journey His journey.

The reader of this story found uniquely in Luke has inside information as to who this man is that has joined Cleopas and his companion. The author wants the reader to know, but is careful to point out that, though it is obvious to those who are reading his letter that the third sojourner is Jesus, the two people living the story are not able to see Him for who He really is. Their eyes have been restrained and they do not know who it is with whom they walk.

If only they knew who they were talking to and walking with as they traveled down that road, they would have asked more questions and made fewer statements. Jesus asks them to recount the story that He Himself knows all too well. They tell him that their master had died at the hands of the enemy. The miracle worker and great teacher had been taken, crucified and sealed in a tomb. "But we were hoping that it was He who was going to redeem Israel" they lamented.

They were not alone in this hope. Luke begins his gospel of Jesus by telling of another couple who had hoped He was the redeemer: Simeon and Anna. When Jesus was just a baby and sacrifices were going to be made at the Temple according to the law of Moses, they both see the child and state that He is the one who will save Israel. The redeemer had arrived and they rejoiced and stated that they can die happy, knowing their brothers and sisters would be saved. Now, at the end of the gospel account, we have two more who, a week earlier, would have declared the same as Simeon and Anna, but now they cannot. As far as they are concerned, Simeon and Anna were wrong. Jesus wasn't the one. How could He be? He is dead. The long weekend was as weary as the road upon which they walked. It seemed to be a hopeless journey to nowhere.

Suddenly, this stranger, whom they thought was clueless, or perhaps lived in a cave somewhere, speaks up and is seemingly quite harsh. "O foolish ones, and slow of heart to believe in all that the prophets have spoken." Their eyes are still restrained and they still do not know who it is they are speaking with. "Ought not the

Christ to have suffered these things and to enter into His glory?", He asked.

So, here our two poor travelers are. Lost, alone, confused and hopeless, they now find a stranger accusing them of not understanding or having faith in the Law and the Prophets. For a moment, the journey may have seemed to have just gotten even longer than it was before He joined them. It was bad enough that their friend and master was dead, but now this unknown man from nowhere is leveling accusations against them.

But then, the hidden Jesus starts at the very beginning, with Moses and all the Prophets to tell them about the Christ- the one they had been waiting on; the one on whom Simeon and Anna had placed their hope; the one on whom Cleopas and his companion had placed their hope: on Jesus Himself - the world's true Messiah.

One might wonder why Jesus did what He did. Why start with Moses and the Prophets? Why not, instead, come to them boldly? What is the point in hiding and restraining their eyes? Or better still, why not come to them performing miracles? Why not come on a cloud into their presence, with trumpets and choirs of angels?

No, Jesus deliberately comes to them in hiding. He chooses to reveal Himself, not through miracles and might, but through the ancient and beloved scripture they had always trusted. Slowly and meticulously, Jesus takes them on a separate journey, perhaps just as turn-filled and rocky, through the Torah, Prophets and Psalms, showing them at every turn of the Old Testament road why it is the Christ had to suffer and die to enter into His glory.

Evening catches up with them, and Jesus seems to have no plan to stay. Places to go and people to see. They compel Him to stay with them at their home in Emmaus. The two travelers would later talk about how their hearts burned within them as they traveled down the road with this stranger. Hearts that burned as He opened up the scripture to them. They sensed that there was something different about this man who guided them through their beloved and sacred texts, but they just couldn't see what it was. And it was there at the table that Jesus, like He had done so often before, took the bread, blessed it and broke it. When He had done this, their eyes were opened and they knew Him. And just as suddenly as He had appeared to them, He left.

What it must have been like to be one of those two travelers on the road! At long last, their "eyes were opened" and they knew Jesus. Interestingly, the phrasing here in Luke 24:31 is word for word what is found in Genesis 3:7.[2] Here, mankind, at the fall, had their eyes opened to see and know their nakedness. While their eyes were opened and they saw their

---

[2] Dane C. Ortlund, Jets 5314 "And Their Eyes Were Opened, And They Knew", Dec 2010, 717-28.

shame, they found that their eyes were closed to another; closed to God Himself. They are now expelled from the garden, from the very presence of God. God is now hidden from them, just out of reach and sight. But now, Jesus has done the great reversal. Now, the eyes of mankind can be opened so that we can see and know Him.

As we travel down the road of our lives, we too need to have our eyes opened. It seems that while we might long to see Jesus do miracles and wonders in our lives, He chooses to reveal Himself to us in much subtler ways. He chooses Jewish scripture and shared meals of communion, above all other avenues, to open our eyes and our understanding.

Indeed, it is Luke who uniquely tells us in 16:19-31, that there are no miracles that can help us to understand, repent and believe. There aren't any signs or wonders that can fully open our eyes and deepen our knowledge. Jesus says that the best way to know Him is to first hear Moses and the prophets.

So, here we stand. A lot has happened since Jesus met those two on the road and broke bread in their home in that small, unknown town seven miles outside of Jerusalem. Christianity has gone through several phases of growth and change, and not all of them have been pleasant, pretty or perfect. And while many of us read the Emmaus road story and long for that same burning to be in our hearts, very few of us are willing to sit in communion with Christ's body and start at Moses and the Prophets and work our way through until we see Him more clearly.

However, this is the call that Jesus, the one on whom our hopes are found, has made to us. Throughout all of the gospels, Jesus beckons us to go back to Moses and find Him. Return to the Psalms and find the Messiah. He tells us to go back through the prophets, and there find the Christ of God.

Martin Luther, in his work *Preface to the Old Testament*, wrote that we should see the swaddling cloths that wrapped the baby Jesus as symbolizing the Old Testament itself. As we study the ancient texts and look more deeply into the swaddling cloths, we will find the Christ child wrapped inside. Luther says it best, "Simple and lowly are these swaddling cloths, but dear is the treasure, Christ, who lies in them."[3] Wrapped in the Law, Psalms and Prophets is Jesus, the redeemer, the greatest treasure ever sought.

Together, we will meticulously and carefully unwrap the swaddling cloths of the Old Testament, specifically the feasts and celebrations, and discover inside their texts the very Lord we worship and put our hope in. Jesus says, "For if you believed Moses, you would believe me, for he wrote about me."[4] Let us journey down the path together. May our eyes be opened so that

[3] Richard B. Hays, Reading Backwards (SPCK, Baylor University Press, 2014, 2015) p. 1.
[4] John 5:46, NKJV

we can see and know Him more fully through the ancient festivals that, ultimately, celebrated Him.

Chapter Two

The Transfiguration of the Law & Prophets

Luke 9:33, 35

"Master, it is good for us to be here, and let us make three tabernacles: one for You, one for Moses and one for Elijah" – not knowing what he was saying

And a voice came out of the cloud, saying, "This is my beloved Son. Hear Him!"

"Get behind me Satan!" The words kept ringing in his ears. Right there, in front of this man's friends and fellow followers, Jesus turned His back on him, Simon Peter, one of His first disciples, and accused him of thinking like a man, not like God. He even calls him Satan, the great accuser. Peter just couldn't stop thinking about it. It just didn't make any sense. He had given up everything to follow his friend. He left his boat, livelihood, family and every dream he had ever had for the future on the shores of Lake Gennesaret to follow Jesus. Peter was the only one bold enough to answer Jesus' challenging question: "Who do you say that I am?" He answered correctly and courageously, "You are the Christ."

How could the only person who seemed to have understood who Jesus was, moments later, be called Satan? How could he go from getting it so right, to getting it so wrong? There, in the presence of the other 11 and their Lord, Peter stood alone. The one who was part of what is known as the "inner circle" now stood on the margins. There in the midst of Jesus's closest friends, Peter contemplated and most certainly mourned over the seemingly harsh and uncalled for statement of his teacher.

Only years later would Peter understand. But for now, his confusion, sadness and pain circled around the all-too-well-known phrase, "the Christ". For, though he had said rightly, and perhaps proudly, that Jesus was the Christ, he didn't know what it meant. He had in mind the things of men, not of God. He only thought he knew what it meant to follow the Christ, but Jesus was about to reveal a startling and painful truth. It was a truth Peter should have known, but it had been hidden from him. In fact, it had been hidden from everyone.

Before Jesus spoke these words to Peter, He had been teaching them what it truly meant to be the Messiah. Though men might think that the Messiah had come to rule in worldly power and might, crushing the enemy, Rome, under the weight of military strength and assuming the throne in glory and splendor, Jesus told quite a different tale, completely dissimilar in every way to the thoughts of men.

On the heels of Peter's confession of Jesus as Messiah, Jesus told the twelve disciples a secret. It was God's secret, foretold thousands of years prior, in a variety of ways and passages, in their scriptures. A secret that, though spoken of often, was never understood. The Christ must suffer, be rejected and be killed. No great armies would follow Him into battle. No crown of glory would ever sit upon His head. Perhaps worse, no throne to the left or right where His disciples might reign. No, He must die and sit in a tomb for three days. He told them that He would rise again once the days of death were complete, but the teaching was not understood. Indeed, none of what He said that day was understood.

Peter, thinking that Jesus had lost His mind, pulls Him aside and rebukes Him. One can only imagine what Peter might have said. "Look here. I gave up everything to follow you. Don't ruin it with crazy talk. Don't you understand the scripture? You are confusing and discouraging everyone!" Finally, Jesus had heard enough. "Get behind me, Satan!" he exclaimed. "You have the thinking of a mere man, not God."

The picture Jesus was about to paint for them was ominous indeed. This road He would travel that eventually ended at death was the road every person must travel if they are to be His followers.

Every person who wishes to be a part of His revolution must despise his own life, take up a cross and drag it along the same path that the Christ walked. The follower is called to lose himself completely and utterly, for this is what it means to think and be like the Christ. This is what it means to think and live out the thoughts of God. This is what it means to live the secret God had been whispering throughout the Old Testament. Jesus has a plan to reveal this truth, even more fully, to His first disciples, Peter, James and John.

The disciples were accustomed to Jesus going off alone to pray. Jesus would go alone, away from the crowds and His twelve disciples, and speak with His Father. But today was different. Six days after hearing Jesus' difficult teaching, these three were to go with Him. Jesus pointed off in the distance, showing them a high mountain peak and invited them to go with Him to pray. There, on that high and lonely mountain, was something they needed to see. There was a voice they needed to hear.

Peter, James, John and Jesus walk up the mountain together. The journey to the top was tiresome; the heat of the day and the arduous ascent had emptied the three disciples of all their energy. Jesus prays to His Father, but the others are on the verge of collapse and fall asleep. Perhaps they had found a nice, shady spot under a tree where they found respite from the sun and refreshing from a gentle breeze.

While they slept, Jesus speaks with His Father. As He prays, He begins to change. The appearance of His face is altered, shining brilliantly like the sun in the heavens. His clothes are made white and glistening, like the light of the western ocean at the setting sun. He is shining so brightly that the three are awakened and tremble in fear at the sight. They have seen Jesus in glory. Moses had a similar experience on another mountain; his face glowed with God's glory.[5] But, unlike Moses, the very glory of God Himself was emanating from Jesus, powerful and strong.

---

[5] Exodus 34:29-35

As they awaken from their slumber and realize what is going on, they see that Jesus is not alone. They might have fallen asleep, but there were two others with Him on the mountain that day. Somehow, quite mysteriously, the three disciples know who these other two men are. It is Moses and Elijah. Moses, the great law giver and deliverer. Elijah, the prophet who symbolized all the prophets who ever came before or after him. They were there with Jesus, having the strangest of conversations. They were talking to Jesus about His impending death[6] that was soon to take place in Jerusalem.

---

[6] The Greek word Luke chooses is "exodo", indicating Jesus will bring about a new kind of deliverance through His death.

The disciples are privy to this conversation between the Christ, the Law and the Prophets. They look at each other in fear and confusion, squinting at each other in the brightness of their Lord. "Why does Jesus look this way?", they must have pondered. When they hear the conversation, they are even more troubled. Peter, most of all, had to have been completely crushed. They were talking about how Jesus was going to die. He must have replayed the word, "Get behind me Satan" over and over again as the heavenly dialogue traveled across the beams of light and rang in his ears.

Could it be that, somehow, the Law and the Prophets spoke of the death of the Messiah? Could it be that the very mention of any other plan came from the heart and imagination of Satan himself? This seems to be exactly the case. Here, in the glory of God, the only conversation being had is that of the death of Jesus.

Peter, in his bewilderment and need to always say something, voices the idea that they should build three tabernacles in honor of this occasion. Three altars for three great and worthy men of God. Moses and Elijah are just about to leave as Peter announces his plan.

Suddenly, a cloud came and overshadowed them. It was bright and daunting, striking fear in the hearts of the disciples. Moses and Elijah stay with them in the bright and radiating cloud. James and John must have thought to themselves, "Why Peter, why?" Like children, they must have thought that Peter had single-handedly condemned them all. While we do not know what they thought was going to happen next, it is almost a forgone certainty that God's next move was unexpected.

God speaks to them from the bright and shining cloud, in the presence of Moses, Elijah and the Messiah, and tells them that Jesus is His beloved son. They are to listen to Him. Just as suddenly as the cloud had appeared, in the blinking of an eye, it was gone. They find themselves alone with Jesus and He appears the way they always knew Him. They also find themselves, once again, wondering what it all might mean.

Matthew, Mark and Luke all tell of this event in their gospels, with only slight variations as to the details. Why is this event so important? What does this have to do with seeing Jesus in the ancient Jewish scriptures?

The first thing to note is that the followers of Jesus, even those closest to Him, did not truly understand the Law of Moses or the Prophets. Yes, Peter, James and John left everything that day at the lake and started a new life, but they lacked understanding. And Peter certainly did get it right when he declared Jesus to be the Christ, but as we have seen, he was only right in title, not in vocation. He truly did not know what that meant. In his mind, and most certainly in the minds of the less talkative disciples, the Christ would not die. The very idea was absurd! Did not the scriptures state that the Messiah would have an everlasting throne? A dead Messiah just isn't coherent with their understanding of the Law and Prophets. Yet we see both Moses and Elijah, the greatest representatives of the Law and Prophets ever given by God, speaking to Jesus about this very immanent event. Jesus, the Christ, was to die.

Here, we literally see the Law and Prophets speaking of the death of Jesus. Peter, James, John, and nearly everyone else, had not been hearing the Old Testament correctly. Yes, their eyes had been shut to this fact. But now they are faced with an undeniable truth. What shall they do with this newfound verity? At this point, they still do not know. You could say that their eyes and ears had been restrained; they just couldn't understand it. As they go down the mountain, they are still debating the meaning of everything they had experienced.

Secondly, we should also pay especially close attention to the cloud and the voice. As stated earlier, Moses experienced God in the cloud and his face radiated with the glory of God. In the cloud, he heard God's voice and received His law. Now, once again, the cloud has come and the voice has spoken. The words couldn't have been any clearer. You may want to build tabernacles to all three persons present here, but there is only one voice you should listen to; the voice of my beloved son, Jesus. Only in Him will it all make sense and have meaning.

For so long, the children of Israel had searched through the scriptures, trying to understand the plans and purposes of God. They studied intently the words of Moses, the Prophets and the Psalms but seemingly to no avail. On this mountain we see that, though the Law and Prophets speak of the Christ and His death, the understanding of the disciples is incomplete at best. If they truly want to honor the Law and the Prophets, they must listen to Jesus. Listening to Him is the only way to understanding. The Old Testament has been transfigured and made to shine in and through Jesus. Only in Him is comprehension given.

So, we find ourselves once again at the end of Luke with the two travelers, Cleopas and his companion. As it is stated in Luke 24: 45, "And He opened their understanding, that they might comprehend the scriptures." There with Peter, James, John and the other disciples, He started, just as He had with Cleopas and his friend, from Genesis to Malachi and showed them the true meaning of their sacred writings.

It should be clear to us by now that not only should we, but we must, return to the Old Testament to better understand Jesus. Its speaks about Him. Jesus Himself uses these inspired passages to teach His disciples about His true nature. They should not be ignored or pushed aside.

Of course, the opposite is also true: we must turn to Jesus to understand the Old Testament. If we are to truly understand the Passover, the Booths, the Weeks and the other festivals, we must understand them in light of Jesus. Yes, we are to "listen to Him".

Part Two

The Celebrations of Jesus

Chapter Three

The New Passover

Exodus 12:13

Now the blood shall be a sign for you on the houses where you are. And when I see the blood, I will pass over you; and the plague shall not be on you to destroy you when I strike the land of Egypt.

The children of Israel could be found in their homes, sheltered from the heavy and burdensome darkness that filled the air. There, in their houses, they sat in the only light that could be seen in all the land. Just beyond the door, outside the window, was a plague from God Himself. The God we know as light had ushered in utter darkness, thick and relentlessly present.

The ninth plague had been issued. Eight other plagues had come and gone, each time with a plea from the Jewish leaders, Moses and Aaron, that Pharaoh release the children of God so they could serve their Lord. Each plea was met with a hard-hearted Pharaoh, refusing to let go of

his slaves: God's first born child, Israel,
Pharaoh thought, belonged to him.

And there, in the African country of
Egypt, a black, heavy darkness fell upon
the land; so thick was this darkness that it
could be felt in the hands of their
oppressors. For three days, the Egyptians
stayed in their homes, not moving from the
spot they found themselves in when the
darkness fell upon them. Covered in a
black, impenetrable night they waited, not
knowing if and when it would end. The
land of Egypt had become like the night sky
and the Israelites had become like stars. In
the dwellings of the enslaved Jews, their
homes shined bright with light. Darkness
had not overcome them. To the contrary,

the light was not able to be extinguished by the darkness.[7]

The ruler of Egypt had been through eight other plagues. The Nile river that had swallowed up the Jewish baby boys had been turned to blood. Frogs, lice, flies and pestilence filled the land, but no freedom was to be given. Boils, hail and locusts came, but with every wonder put on display by God through His chosen freedom bringers, the heart of Pharaoh grew harder and more callous. He had been blinded by his pride, but he was about to be humbled. Before any plague had come to pass, God had warned Pharaoh that if he did not let His firstborn

---

[7] The Gospel of John makes great use of this imagery, not least in the first chapter of his account.

child - as He lovingly called Israel - go, God himself would remove all the first born from Pharaoh's land. Tragically, the promised death of God was about to come to bear.

Though the darkness had subsided, a greater darkness was about to be inflicted. At midnight, God himself went in to the midst of the Egyptians. And there, while the Egyptians slumbered in their homes, death came upon them and their families. The destroyer of God had been unleashed in the land and the firstborn from every Egyptian home, from king to prisoner, died that night.[8] Even the beasts of the field lie dead on the ground. No

---

[8] The death of the firstborn is directly connected to the slaughter of the Israelite boys in Exodus 4:25.

firstborn among them had been spared. The weeping of the families was a noise unlike any ever heard in the country, echoing off the walls and traveling through the roads and passage ways of that ancient territory.

However, as God moved through the land, He did not kill every firstborn in every home. His firstborn son found himself safe. Their doorposts and lintels were painted with the blood of a sacrificed firstborn lamb, a lamb without blemish or spot. God's destroyer saw the blood and passed over their homes. They had been spared God's final act of judgement by the blood of the lamb.

This was the only plague where God required action from His children. Every other wonder God had wrought, He did while the children of Israel stood back and watched. They were safe every time. This plague was different. If they wanted to survive the night, they had to celebrate a new feast, the first ever prescribed: The Passover.

At twilight, while the sun was setting at the end of the day, the Jews were instructed to kill the firstborn lamb, one without blemish, and sacrifice it to the Lord. They took a hyssop branch, dipped it into the blood of the sacrificed lamb that had been captured in a basin and struck the doorposts and lentils of their homes with the branch, thereby putting the blood on the entry ways. They also ate unleavened bread with bitter herbs this night, under the door ways with the blood.

As the destroyer of God swept across the city, the blood of the lamb was a clear sign that this house was not to be touched. This house was filled with God's children.

The Feast of the Passover had been marvelously established. Once a year, on the first day of the year, just as God had commanded them as the power of Egypt over them faded into the twilight skies, the Jews would come together and celebrate this event and remember the day that God delivered them from a land of death to a land of life. This was the day when new life could spring forth, for death had passed them by.[9]

The feast was celebrated throughout Jewish history, but seemingly it was never more meaningful than when the children of Israel found themselves in slavery or with foreign oppressors looming on the horizon. In these moments, they longed to once again be set free.

One such occasion is noted in 2 Kings 23. The Israelites were living in the waning power of their captors, the Assyrians. As the Assyrian power was weakening, Israel found themselves able to rule themselves will less influence from

---

[9] The Hebrew word for Passover, Pesach means "to spring or jump, pass over" Barney Kasdan, "God's Appointed Times", p 26, Messianic Jewish Publishers 1993.

foreign powers. Their king, Josiah, led a refreshing movement to restore the Temple to its former glory and splendor, removing the idols that had been put there by his family that came before him. Once the Temple had been cleansed, Josiah celebrated the Feast of the Passover as it had never been done before.[10]

The next mention of this Passover being celebrated is found in the book of Ezra.[11] The Assyrian oppressors were eventually defeated by the even more wicked Babylonians and the children of Israel were taken once again into captivity. This time, at the hands of their Babylonian King, Nebuchadnezzar, their temple was

---

[10] 2 Chronicles 35:18
[11] Ezra 6:19ff

completely destroyed. The entire city of Jerusalem was laid waste and its inhabitants were taken into slavery, into the land of Babylon.

It was there in Babylon that the prophet Ezekiel saw a vision and prophesied about a time when the land and Temple would be fully realized and restored and the feasts would once again be celebrated. His vision ends with the word of God saying, "THE LORD IS THERE". It was an appropriate ending, for the Lord seemed to be missing and was desperately needed to return.

After 70 years in Babylonian captivity, the Persians defeated the Babylonians and now ruled the entire Near East. The Jews were allowed to return to their land and rebuild their Temple. Once the Temple was completed, the children of Israel rejoiced. God had turned the hearts of the rulers of Persia, king Cyrus, king Darius and king Artaxerxes, towards Him and towards His people. With the Temple rebuilt, the first celebration to be had was that of Passover. The children killed the lamb, ate the unleavened bread and bitter herbs in their homes and remembered the God who delivers them from slavery when they cry out to and follow Him.[12] The Lord had made their hearts joyful once again.[13]

If only the story had ended there. But it does not. When the Greeks came into power under Alexander the Great, and

---

[12] The accounts of the return from exile can be read in Ezra and Nehemiah.
[13] Ezra 6:22

then the Romans after them, the Israelites were completely confused and devastated. The feast that celebrated a liberating God must have been celebrated during this time with bitter-sweet sentiment. In fact, after the celebration mentioned in Ezra, the Old Testament makes gives no further examples of another one being celebrated. This isn't to say that they stopped celebrating Passover. This certainly wouldn't have been the case. But the celebrations were different now. The Passover was now performed, not just looking and celebrating the past, but also done while looking ahead to a bright, hoped-for future. Though no longer under Babylonian rule, they were still waiting for the vision that Ezekiel saw to come true. When would it all be fulfilled? When would they once again see the Temple filled with the very glory of God, the same glory that lead them through the wilderness with Moses? This longing for another Passover carries right through into the New Testament.

Interestingly, Matthew, Mark and Luke only mention the Passover feast one time. Those of us familiar with the story know it all too well. Jesus is in the upper room with his twelve disciples. Jesus shares His heart with them, telling them that He has longed for this day to come. It has been His desire to share this Passover meal with His friends and followers; breaking bread with them and drinking wine with them. On this evening, Jesus does something quite unexpected in the presence of His disciples. He reorients the entire feast around Himself and His own actions yet to be performed.

Their Lord and Master begins to reveal a deeper meaning of everything that the feast had ever signified to them. Jesus tells them that the bread is His body, the wine is His blood. The four cups of wine, while not part of the original Passover celebrations, were added to remember the four promises God made to Israel, before a single plague had been issued.[14] The promises of the wine remembered were: (1) Israel being set apart, (2) set free, (3) redeemed and (4) made God's family.[15] Now, at the Last Supper, the wine is

---

[14] See Kasdan, God's Appointed Times
[15] Exodus 6:6-7

representing the blood of Jesus Himself. Blood that will forgive sins and bring His people back from the slavery and exile that disobedience to God always brings to bear. The promises are fulfilled again and more fully in Jesus's blood.

The Feast of Unleavened Bread, once celebrated to remind them of the haste with which God came and freed them now also points to the body of Jesus, needing to be broken for their liberation. The bitter herbs into which the Jews would dip the bread, once representing the oppression and bitter treatment of slavery in Egypt, was now refocused on the sin that Jesus Himself would bear upon His body.

In all of these ways, Jesus is telling His followers that the Passover, at its deepest and most real level, was always about Him. The bitterness of slavery needed to be carried away. A perfect sacrifice would need to be made: a firstborn and blameless sacrifice. This was the ultimate cost for ultimate freedom.

We have said in the previous chapter that the eyes of the followers of Jesus had been closed or restrained and they were unable to understand His teachings and actions. They were unable to discern the Law and the Prophets. So, here again we see that even the very celebration of Passover had not been fully understood. They had been celebrating Jesus throughout their history, but they did not know it. In Jesus, the long-awaited Passover had arrived. Through the breaking of His body and the pouring out of His blood, the children of God would be led out of the land of slavery and into the promised land of freedom.

However, there seems to be one part of the feast that is glaringly missing from the first three gospel accounts. What of the lamb of the Passover? Mathew, Mark and Luke make no mention of the lamb in any of their Passover feast accounts. How is the lamb of Passover to be understood? If we have grown up in church, we do not even think to ask this question. Our minds, as if set on autopilot, intuitively know that the lamb is Jesus Himself. But, from what source would we get such a concept?

71

And what about John? What might he have to add to our understanding of the Passover feast and its reorientation and redefinition in Jesus the Christ? It is to this gospel account that we now turn.

Perhaps as interesting as the fact that Matthew, Mark and Luke only mention the Passover once, is the fact that John repeatedly speaks of the events surrounding this great feast. In fact, he speaks of the Passover in seven different chapters, perhaps eight if we conclude that chapter five is referring to the Passover. It appears that John is retelling the entire story of Jesus through the eyes of someone who has come to understand what the Passover is truly all about. He recounts the events through the understanding that

Jesus is the Passover of God! Now, with the Passover redefined, John sees this as a vital recognition to understanding Jesus, His actions and His teachings.

In this regard, John hits the ground running. Before we are even through the first chapter, Jesus is identified by His cousin, John the Baptist, two times as the Lamb of God. Perhaps oddly, after chapter one, John never mentions Jesus by this title again. It is as If John is inviting us to explore, through his creative telling of the Jesus story, how it is that Jesus truly is the great Passover Lamb of God.

Our first encounter with Jesus during Passover in John is in chapter two. John tells us that the Passover is at hand when Jesus enters the temple. He sees the merchants and money changers and drives them out with a whip. Before Jesus, other Israelite kings and leaders had done similar actions. Josiah cleansed the Temple, just before celebrating this appointed time of the Passover. The Maccabean leaders had also cleansed the Temple after their famous revolt and short-lived victory. Could it be that this Lamb of God was here to deliver His children out of captivity? Could it be that He had come to purify the Temple and once again celebrate Passover as never done before?

We see the Lamb again in chapter five, during the Passover.[16] Here, He encounters a man who has been sick for 38

---

[16] There is debate as to what "the/a feast" actually refers to, but the description, though brief, and timeline indicate that this was a Passover feast.

years, his body had been held captive, but on the Sabbath, the man finds rest. He finds deliverance. This is the same passage where Jesus tells those who oppose Him that His works are like a bright light burning, but they do not see it. He tells them that, though they claim to love Moses and follow him, it is not so. Moses wrote about Him, and they do not believe Him. Could it be that when Moses wrote about the Passover lamb, he was writing about Jesus? The lamb that freed them was walking in their midst, but they did not see or recognize Him. Indeed, the lamb had come unto His own, but His own did not receive Him.

We now turn to chapter six. John tells us that the Passover Feast is about to take place. Jesus has been teaching a group of about 5000 people, and He wants to feed them. Jesus instructs His disciples have them sit down in a field. Jesus feeds the famished crowd as much as they want with only five loaves of bread and two fish. Before they go to the Feast, Jesus tells them that He is the true bread that comes from heaven. Just as God had brought the children out of the land of Egypt and fed them in the desert, now Jesus was going to lead them out of bondage and feed them bread that is greater than the manna that Moses gave: true bread from heaven.

There is only one Passover Feast left. John mentions it in chapter 11 and continues to refer to it all the way to chapter 19. With each passing account of the events as they unfold, this final Passover draws ever nearer. As it draws near, the Lamb of God claims to be the resurrection and life that the Jews believed would be theirs in the final day of judgement. Jesus says that what they have been hoping to receive at the end, He has delivered to them. He brought the end of the story to the middle. His friend Lazarus is raised from the dead. The oppressor called death is being defeated.

In chapter 12, Jesus reminds His audience that He has come as light in the darkness. We need only remember the plague of darkness to see the allusion. Just days before the Passover, the enemies of God sat in darkness while His firstborn son, Israel, sat in homes filled with light. Jesus invites them to hear Him, believe Him and come into His lighted house surrounded by darkness.   Passover is just around the corner. The lamb is about to be sacrificed.

As the celebration draws closer, John tells us of a conversation unlike any other found in the other Gospel accounts. Jesus washes the disciples' feet, tells them to love one another and informs them that the time has come for Him to be betrayed into the hands of sinners.

There in Jerusalem, abandoned by most, denied by one and betrayed by another, just before the Passover was to begin, Jesus, the Lamb of God, was nailed to a cross. He breathed His last breath of air and His heart failed to beat. It was the price of freedom. The lamb had to be slain

so the destroyer wouldn't harm any of
God's children. On a hill called Golgotha,
the Lamb of God was killed. The Passover
had been fulfilled.

For John, everything Jesus did was,
in some way, reshaping the ancient stories
he knew so well. For years, John had
celebrated the Passover with his family
and never once did he imagine that the
Feast was actually a great "looking
forward" to the fate of the Messiah. No
one had imagined it. But it was God's plan
all along. Once it was completed, it all
seemed so clear. The Passover, from the
very beginning, had always been a
celebration of Jesus. His body, His blood
and His sacrifice had redeemed a lost and
enslaved people. If sin had caused death

and exile, the Passover redeems those in exile and conquers death.

Death will pass us over. The entry ways to our homes have been brushed with the blood of the Lamb of God. We belong to Him. Pharaoh has let us go, that we may serve our God. Amen.

The Scriptures & Occasion of Feast

Leviticus 23:5-8

- Celebrated on the 14th day of the 1st month, followed by Feast of Unleavened Bread on 15th day of 1st month
- 1st Day of Spring (in Hebrew, word means to "spring, jump or pass over")

Exodus 12.13

- Blood of the Lamb on door posts, I will "pass over", no plague will touch you

1 Corinthians 5:6-8

- Christ is our Passover, in Him we rid ourselves of the leaven of sin (vs

8, we keep the feast with sincerity and truth)

1 Corinthians 10:1-13

o *After the Passover and Exodus, people tempted and fall into sin and idolatry, but God has given us a Passover (vs 13, way of escape)*

Chapter Four

The Firstfruits

John 12:24

Unless a grain of wheat falls into the ground and dies, it remains alone: but if it dies, it produces much grain.

It is early in the morning. The air is crisp and cool as the sun rises over the eastern skies of Israel. It was the beginning of Spring, and the signs of life after a long winter were everywhere.   Trees were turning green and flowers were sprouting from the once cold and frozen ground. As the sun's rays penetrate through the morning clouds and fog, the children of God are joyfully working in the fields. They are gathering up a small part of barley, the earliest crop to be harvested, so that it can be offered to God at the Temple.

Once collected, they would all rush from the fields to a spot, just outside of the city of Jerusalem, to meet the priest. There, at the edge of the city, the priest would come and lead them in a celebration of joy and expectation. With the priest were a choir and dancers. Together they would sing and dance their way to the Temple.[17] The Feast of the Early Firstfruits had begun.

This celebration was one of the few that was performed deliberating in anticipation of the next feast, Pentecost, also known as the Feast of the Latter Firstfruits. The children of Israel would keep this ordinance from God, celebrating that since the early harvest of barley had come, they could rest confident in the fact that the next harvest was on the way. After winter passed, it was exciting to see God provide for their needs. The feast was

---

[17] God's Appointed Times, Kasdan, pg. 40.

a sign of hope: hope for today and an even greater hope for the future.

The Feast of the Early Firstfruits was celebrated right after Passover. Within the gospel accounts, it is eclipsed by the celebration that came before and is therefore never mentioned specifically in any of the gospels. However, in the Gospel of John, Jesus makes a very cryptic statement that can only be understood in light of this feast. He says that unless a grain is buried and dies, it will never bear fruit. But, if it is buried and dead, only then will it bear much fruit. Here, Jesus says that this is how His life, or more appropriately, His death, is to be understood.

Jesus says that He is about to be killed and be buried. Just like the grains of the first harvest of barley were once a single seed, so He too is also a single seed. But as the Jews knew all too well, a single seed once buried would never remain the same. In order to bring life in abundance, it first had to die. Jesus mysteriously relates this common occurrence in nature to His own life and death.

Jesus makes this statement just days before the Feast is to be celebrated. He says that His appointed time has come, His hour is at hand. In other words, He is the firstfruits and unless He dies, there will be no early harvest. And if there is no early harvest, there cannot be a later harvest either.

As we saw with the transfiguration and the comments Peter made leading up to this event, the disciples were not ready to see their friend be buried in the ground. Death was not part of their plan. But it was part of God's plan from the very beginning. And here, in the ancient celebration, we see that God had been indicating all along how the plan would unfold.

With every spring time festival-though unbeknownst to the celebrating crowds-they danced and sang their way to the Temple in honor of the one who would one day be buried in the ground so that they might live. They celebrated the resurrection of Jesus from the dead. His resurrection gave hope for today: resurrected life is springing out of the ground. His resurrection gives hope for tomorrow: there is another harvest, an even greater harvest, on the way. What happened with one man at the early harvest, would happen to faithful humanity at the latter.

The apostle Paul makes this connection abundantly clear in 1 Corinthians 15:23. Here Paul is explaining to the believers in Corinth the meaning of Christ's resurrection. The Christians in this town seem to be in danger of giving up in the hope of the resurrection. In fact, many there seem to have stopped believing in the resurrection from the dead. Paul is understandably compelled to correct this major misstep. Here, he gives the longest and best explanation of what the resurrection is all about. The hope in the future harvest depends on there being an early harvest. "Christ the firstfruits", he explains. "Afterward, those who are Christ's." Just as the early harvest pointed forward to the latter, so does Christ's resurrection point forward to yet another, even greater harvest.

This simple feast had all along been part of God's plan, subtle and often hidden from their understanding, to celebrate the day when His own Son would die, be buried and raise to new life. "This is how it had to be", Jesus would say. "This is what the Law and the Prophets have been talking about all along." It was part of their life, culture and religion, but they didn't see it until they saw and knew Him first.

Woven into the very fabric of our world, right in front of our very eyes, God had hidden His eternal plan. From the very beginning, in the book of Genesis, when God spoke of "seedtime and harvest", He had the celebration of His Son in mind. May the Feast of the Firstfruits ever remind us of Him. Jesus has risen from the dead. We, too, shall rise.

Scriptures and Occasion of Feast

Leviticus 23:9-14

- Celebrated right after the Passover
- Remembering the blessing of the Promised land with the early harvest of barley
- Looks forward to the Latterfruits harvest yet to come

1 Corinthians 15:20-23

- Christ risen from the dead as the Firstfruits, our resurrection to follow as the Latter Fruits harvest

Romans 8:23

- Holy Spirit in us, guiding us, is the Firstfruit as we look forward to the Latter Fruit harvest: the redemption of our bodies

Chapter Five

The Latter Firstfruits

Leviticus 23:15-16

"You shall count seven full weeks from the day after the Sabbath, from the day that you brought the sheaf of the wave offering. [16] You shall count fifty days to the day after the seventh Sabbath. Then you shall present a grain offering of new grain to the LORD.

"The commandment that was meant to bring life, I found to bring only death." As a Jewish believer in Christ, having just returned to Rome from the banishment enforced by Emperor Claudius, you hear these words from Paul in complete disbelief and anger. "How can anyone say such a thing about the holy scripture from God?" It is bad enough that the Gentile believers have been making scurrilous remarks regarding your beloved texts, but now even Paul, formerly part of the elite, is seemingly siding with them.

But as he continues to explain himself, you suddenly find yourself confessing, much to your own dislike, that he is simply telling a hard truth. The commands of God were indeed powerless to save you. Instead of looking back on the law with endearment, you, for the first time, sit back and agree with his nearly heretical comment. For you too, when you remember your own life before coming to know the Messiah, were powerless to live the life of a light shining in the darkness the Creator of everything had called you to. The very word that had called you to be a guide to the blind, an instructor of the foolish and a teacher of babes also seems to scream at you at every turn of life that you have fallen short. You have failed. Instead of living your life to God, you know that you have lived your life to flesh. Even at your best, you find yourself looking at the good law of God and collapsing under the weight of your shortcomings. In your mind, you long to live the law, but in your body you cannot.

In this moment, you regret every Feast of Weeks you have ever celebrated. It was seven weeks from Egypt to Mount Sinai. These seven weeks were to be celebrated with joy that the good and holy command of God had finally come to man. You remember rejoicing as you came into the city with your offerings of wheat. You remember the absolute eagerness of your family as preparations were being made. If the early fruits were in part a celebration of God's liberation, then surely the latter was meant to celebrate the means by which you could live that freedom out in holiness. But now, the words that angered you only sadden your heart. All the years of celebrating the word of God seem to be a waste, not because of the command, but because of your failures. As you listen further, you find yourself in tears as Paul sorrowfully states, "O wretched and awful man that I am! Who will deliver me from this flesh of death?"[18]

Then, your tears change from gloom to grateful gladness. You are, after all, a Messianic Jew. You have put your faith in Jesus, the Messiah of God, King of all the world. In Him you have crossed yet again the Red Sea that once led to the powerless, yet holy, law of God, but now leads to the Spirit. You cry out at the reading of Romans, "Amen!", as you hear

---

[18] Romans 7 isn't a biographical description of Paul's life, but rather a description of life under a holy law that one has failed to keep.

the next sentence: "Therefore, there isn't any condemnation for those who are in the Messiah Jesus. You do not walk in the flesh any longer, but instead you walk according to the Spirit." You rejoice and celebrate a new Pentecost, a new Feast of Weeks, as you recognize that the sin that lives in the flesh cannot and does not live in the Spirit. You are free at last.

The Feast of Weeks is so full of meaning that it is hard to contain. As pointed out in the previous chapter, Jesus' resurrection is like the early harvest and the great day of resurrection is the latter. This is an awesome truth, deeply imbedded in creation itself.

However, The Feast of Weeks is not only a celebration of the hoped-for future.

It is a celebration of the here-and-now. It is a joyful celebration of that joyful moment when God poured out His Spirit on all mankind, allowing His human creation to thrive and reign in life as He had always intended.

Here, in Paul's letter to the Romans, very much under the radar, Paul alludes to this great feast so subtly that it rarely is ever even noticed.

However, not all authors are so subtle. Luke make this connection very clearly in the book of Acts. It is there that we see the disciples, under the instruction of Jesus, to wait on The Festival of Weeks - the true festival - to arrive. There in prayerful hiding, they eagerly awaited the revelation of the Spirit of God. And in

Mount Sinai fashion, the room they were in was filled with the sound of a powerful, rushing wind. The room was filled with the Spirit and gifts were given.

As we saw earlier, Jesus is our true Passover. Unlike the seven-week journey of old that led to the Law, this new journey leads to power in the Spirit. It leads to the only power by which you can live for God, a power that the holy law could not provide.

Returning to our first scene in this chapter, you look back on the yearly Festival of Weeks that you have celebrated from youth, but you remember it differently now. Jesus, your true Passover, has not led you to the mountain where the law is given, but rather to the place where

the very Spirit of God dwells. You realize
that you and your people had actually
been celebrating Jesus throughout your
history. You have been celebrating and
longing for the time, found in the Messiah,
where you could cross over to freedom
and find the power of the Spirit that
enables you to live for God and serve Him.

As Ezekiel says in 36:26 and
following, God will put His Spirit within us
and write His law on our hearts. We are
now empowered to live out His law. In
Jesus, The Festival of Weeks has been
fulfilled in us.

Scripture and Occasion of Feast

Leviticus 23:15-21

- ○ *Celebrated seven weeks after Early or Firstfruits with wheat offerings*
- ○ *Sacrifice for sin made (1 male goat and 2 lambs)*
- ○ *Also known as Pentecost or Festival of Weeks*
- ○ *Also celebrated to remember the giving of the law at Mt. Sinai (tradition)*

Nehemiah 10:37

- ○ *Nation of Israel is back from Babylon and the wall is complete. They reinstitute the feasts of Leviticus 23 and give God His Firstfruits with joy*

Acts 2:1-12

○ *Seven weeks after Passover and death, burial and resurrection of Jesus, the new Passover in Christ leads not to the law, but to the Spirit bring poured out on all flesh*

Revelation 14:4

○ *The 144,000 redeemed from the earth were a Firstfruit unto the God and the Lamb*

James 1:18

○ *God has made us His Firstfruits of His creatures*

Chapter Six

The New Trumpets

Matthew 24:31

He will send His angels with a great sound

of a trumpet, and they will gather

together His chosen ones from the four

winds, from one end of heaven to another.

The work is finally complete. Just over seven weeks have gone by, but in many ways it seems as though an entire lifetime has passed. What are you to do now that the work is complete? Your special calling from God, one that started with high risk and was completed in the midst of warring neighbors and enemies who were against you at every turn, is done. How do you commemorate this moment in honor of the God who chose you to do His holy work?

As you, Nehemiah, consider the past several weeks as you built the wall surrounding Jerusalem, defying the odds, you remember what life was like just months before. Many of your brothers were spread across the face of the land.

Some were and are still in Babylon. Others were dwelling in the surrounding cities. Many were there closer to the new temple, built nearly a century before by some of the first to return from Babylonian exile. Now, because of your vision and task from God, the people can come together as one from the ends of the land and worship God in His holy temple. A great regathering of those who were once divided has occurred. If only there were a way, a way devised by God Himself, to celebrate such a momentous occasion?

The nation of Israel gathers outside of the newly built Water Gate. You watch as the people cry out to Ezra, the greatest giver of the law of God since Moses, to deliver to them a word from the God who had freed them from exile and surrounded them with His loving protection.

You watch as Ezra takes advantage of the appointed time, a time that he and few others are aware of, to celebrate this regathering; this new beginning where you and your countrymen can start afresh. It is the first day of the seventh month. God's timing is perfect. Just as prescribed in the ancient texts of generations passed, you come together as one man and celebrate the Feast of Trumpets. It is time to gather together and start anew.

In grateful amazement, you stand with your family and listen to the law be read from morning to mid-day. You bow down your face to the ground, lift your hands toward the heavens and cry out,

"Amen", as Ezra blesses the Lord through the reading. You think to yourself, "Praise God! The exile is over. The trumpet has sounded and God's people, my family, are free and safe. Our weeping has turned to joy. It is time to start again."

In the past, this feast was celebrated as a time of reflection and introspection. It was a New Year: a time to come together and reevaluate life. The sound of the trumpet was a wake-up call to get your life in order. God was going to do a new thing in your life, and this feast was a time to make sure you were ready for what God was going to do.

Unlike Passover or Pentecost, this celebration is not well known to many believers today. In fact, many of the references or allusions in the New Testament to this feast are completely lost. The passage at the start of this chapter is one such reference.

Jesus, when speaking in Matthew 24:29-31, is referring to what was then a very well-known feast and celebration. He tells us that there is a time coming when the powers of this world, in cosmic-collapse/apocalyptic fashion, will fall but that He will begin His new work. The trumpet sound will ring out, sounding the alarm that new movement and work of God is about to begin. He will gather together His people from the ends of the earth and the far reaches of heaven: new creation will begin.

Part of this feast was a recognition that God is King over all the earth. He is the creator of heaven and earth and therefore rules sovereign over all. In this celebration, the people of God would not only celebrate a New Year, but remember how God will renew His creation. Indeed, all of creation will be made new in the "day".

This is why Paul, when speaking of the return of Jesus the Messiah, speaks of His coming as starting with a trumpet. In his first letter to the believers in Thessalonica, he tells them that the Messiah will return to earth, descending from heaven with a shout and the trumpet of God. It is then that the faithful, dead and alive, will receive their renewed bodies. It is at this moment that His people will be gathered together from the ends of creation to one place, as one man, and start afresh.

Since the institution of this feast in Leviticus 23, God had this moment in mind all along. As we have seen in previous chapters (and will see in the subsequent ones as well), each and every Feast of Trumpets ever celebrated were in reality celebrations of Jesus, the Messiah. They were celebrating the moment when Jesus will fulfill the ultimate time when God's people will wholly be gathered as one, the trumpet will sound, justice and mercy will reign and new creation will be fully realized.

As believers in the Messiah, Jesus, we are called to long for the moment when the trumpet of God will resound throughout His creation. We want to feel the vibration pulse through our bodies. We want to experience and be a part of the new creation God is about to usher in. Sound the alarm! Let the trumpet sound be heard! May God reign!

Scriptures and Occasion of Feast

Leviticus 23:23-25

- A High Sabbath (no work performed, regardless of actual day of celebration)
- New Year, celebrated with trumpet blast using the horn of a ram (shofar)
- Trumpet blast served as wake-up call ready one's self for the work of God
- Celebration of the great regathering of God's people to celebrate feast
- Often celebrated in anticipation of God's Judgement

Nehemiah 8

- o *Nation of Israel all gathered together, celebrating the new work God is doing, the New Year and begin to ready themselves to serve God*

Matthew 24:31

- o *God gathers His people together from the ends of the earth at the sound of the shofar*

1 Thessalonians 4:16-18

- o *At the shofar sound, the Messiah, Jesus, will return to earth and gather together His people, living and dead, vindicating them, reigning forever*

Chapter Seven

The New Atonement

Hebrews 4:14

Seeing then that we have a great High Priest who has passed through to the heavens, Jesus the Son of God, let us hold fast our confession...

Forty days have passed since the you and your newly freed loved ones stood at the foot of the mountain. You remember, as if your legs still trembled beneath you, how the mountain shook at the sound of the trumpet. You remember hearing the thundering voice of the Lord reverberate through the encampment as He spoke, giving the ten commandments[19] in your hearing. You recall how you retreated in fear at the sound of His voice, crying out for Moses to speak to God on your behalf.

You looked up and saw that dark clouds of smoke had encompassed Mount Sinai. The one who had led you out of

---

[19] More accurately known as the "ten words".
Exodus 34:28, Deuteronomy 4:13

Egypt, through the Red Sea and safely to the other side, climbed the mountain of God yet another time. You retreated in fear, but he advanced forward, heeding the voice of the One he had met in this very place just one year earlier as the bush burned unconsumed. You watched him ascend and enter into the billows of darkness, slowly ascending out of sight. There, at the base of the mountain, far from the boundary, you waited anxiously for his return.

Day after day and night after night you and your family waited to see him emerge from the fearful, cloud-filled mountain, but Moses tarried longer than you had hoped. The days turned to weeks with still no sign of Moses to be found. You and all the others assumed the worst. "Moses isn't coming back" you thought to yourselves. "The voice that thundered wasn't the true God." You are all on your own.

There, with all hope seemingly gone, at the foot of the threateningly holy place, Aaron, the brother of Moses, assumes command of the multitude of your brothers. Everyone, at his request, hands over their golden jewelry to him so that he can form for them a calf to worship.

You remember that life now felt normal again. In Egypt, all the gods had an image you could bow down to. Now, at long last, you did too. The fear you once felt had subsided. The frightening glory of God, with His voice like that of crashing waters, had become normal, plain, an everyday affair. When you heard Him say, "Have no other gods before me….make no graven images…" you thought He meant it. But with Moses gone, presumably dead, it seemed like it was time to move on and be like everyone else.

And as you feast, dance and praise the false god of gold, Moses reappears suddenly from the mountain. You still remember his face, filled with both horror and anger, as he came out of the smoke that had once concealed him. In his hands were two tablets of stone with writing on both sides. You didn't know it at the time, but on those stone tablets were the very commands you had heard God thunder from the mountain as you scurried away in terror.

In symbolic fashion, Moses dashed the commandments against the rocky soil, shattering them into irreparable pieces. In your heart, you knew that it wasn't Moses who had broken the law: it was you and all those around you. You had failed before you had started. You had only lasted a little over a month before you had managed to lose faith in the God who delivered you. Just a few weeks before you doubted the man of God who had risked everything to bring you out.

Now, you find yourself waiting again as Moses ascends the mountain, one more time, on your behalf. Previous to his final climb, he had moved his tent away from the camp and pleaded on your behalf. His intercession was successful. God gave mercy to the unrepentant. He gave you mercy when you did not deserve it. Now he goes this one last time to renew the covenant and bring the commands once more to the people of God.

This second bringing of the law came to be known as Yom *(day)* Kippur *(atonement)*. It was the day when the people remembered the grace and mercy of God as the mediator went before Him on behalf of an undeserving people. The sins between them and God were removed and atoned for.

This day, sometimes referred to as "the fast",[20] was and is the most solemn

---

[20] This is the only commanded fast

day of the year. It was a high Sabbath, a Sabbath of Sabbaths, on which no work could be performed, regardless of whether or not it was actually a Saturday. The High Priest, on this day and only this day, would enter the Most Holy Place of the tabernacle/temple and make sacrifice to God, and, like Moses on the mountain, intercede for the people. It was time to rest from your labors; rest from the burden of your sin that broke the holy and good commands of God.

Though this most holy of days was certainly celebrated year after year throughout the history of the people of God, we don't actually have a specific recounting of this day of fasting and intercession. We can know it was performed because it was the last celebration in a string of others that are part of the "days of awe", and we do have stories of these feasts being honored. What we do have are instructions that can be found in Leviticus 16 and 23 as well as Numbers 29, but no accounts of the celebration itself being performed. Moses on the mountain is the only recounting we have from ancient history.

In the book of Hebrews,[21] the writer considers the life and work of Jesus through the lens of the Messiah being our true High Priest. Just as Moses was to

---

[21] Hebrews itself is thought to be a sermon given on The Day of Atonement, Bobby Valentine, "Yom Kippur and the New Testament, Jesus leading Worship"
http://stonedcampbelldisciple.com/2016/05/12/yom-kippur-and-the-new-testament-jesus-leading-worship/

bring the people to the land of rest (Sabbath), now Jesus truly brings rest to His people as the true High Priest, chosen by God before the law, just as Melchizedek had been. This High Priest is unlike any other that has ever entered the Most Holy Place. He enters this true place of holiness, as the true High Priest, with the real sacrifice that need only once be made on behalf of an undeserving people. He is the true mediator that gives true peace and rest.

As Bobby Valentine points out, the life we live in Christ is like living The Day of Atonement. We come together at the base of the mountain and wait for Moses to return. We wait outside the temple where the Messiah ascended and eagerly wait for Him to appear. As Hebrews 9:28 states, "He will appear a second time, not to deal with sin, but for salvation." In Him, sin has been dealt with. He has interceded on our behalf. We now wait for Him to return from that heavenly Most Holy Place and give us ultimate rest. The Messiah, Jesus, is our Yom Kippur. He is our Day of Atonement.

As we have seen so many times before, quite unknown to those who celebrated this day, year after year, the people of God gathered together and celebrated Jesus. They longed for the time when the true High Priest would go into the Most Holy Place, offer the true sacrifice once and for all and bring forgiveness and rest. Amen.

Scriptures and Occasion of Feast

Leviticus 23:26-32

- ○ *High Sabbath*
- ○ *The only mandated fast done annually*
- ○ *Atonement made by intercession*
- ○ *Only day of year High Priest could enter the Most Holy Place, or Holy of Holies*

Leviticus 16

- ○ Detailed description given
- ○ 1 goat sacrificed as sin offering to cover sins; 1 goat served as scapegoat. High Priest would lay his hands on the goat, proclaim the sins of the people on it and send it off into the wilderness, showing

that the sins of the people had been carried away

Romans 3:23-26

○ *Jesus given as atonement sacrifice (propitiation), passing over the sins of the people and fulfilling the righteous requirement in the Messiah*

Romans 8:18-24

○ *We eagerly await our future hope, when Jesus is revealed from the Most Holy Place, and thus we are also revealed to all creation and together we all, mankind and all creation, no longer miss the mark*

Hebrews

- ○ *Thought to be a sermon given on the Day of Atonement, entire book puts Jesus at center of Feast*

Chapter Eight

The New Booths

Zechariah 14:16

*And it will come to pass that everyone
who is left of all the nations which came
against Jerusalem shall go up from year to
year to worship the King, the Lord of
hosts, and to keep the Feast of the
Tabernacles*

The city of Jerusalem is abuzz with excitement. As with Passover, so with the Feast of Tabernacles, the people of the nation of Israel travel from far regions of the area to come and celebrate one of the most joyous feasts of the year. It is a time of joy and hope: a time to celebrate the presence of God in His tabernacle as He led the Israelites out of Egypt and through the wilderness. The people lived in tents, and now for seven days, the people of God too would live in tents to commemorate the time.

However, the joy and excitement of this occasion has eluded you and your family. As the time approaches, you, James, brother of Jesus, are both angry and heartbroken. Mockingly, you and your other brothers taunt Jesus, saying, "Why don't you go up for the feast, Jesus? Show everyone just how great you are! Why are you being so secretive?"

Of all the times of the year, this is supposed to be a happy one. The day of fasting just ended 5 days previous. Atonement has been given and it is finally time to rejoice and be glad. But Jesus, your brother, has ruined everything with his constant troublemaking and popularity. "If you are who you say you are, go to the Feast and show the world!"

Jesus tells you to go without him. This appointed time to celebrate is not his time. So you go, hoping no one recognizes you as His brother.

The New Booths

When you arrive, you see countless huts set up all along the streets and byways. You look and appreciate joyfully that all the people, your people, have come to remember what God had done.

As you proceed through the town, you see that there are massively tall towers, reaching high into the sky, with fires burning bright. Even in the evening, there is light to guide your way. You are reminded of what Zechariah said: "In that day, there will be no light. The lights will diminish and it will be only day, no night." You look forward to the last day of the feast, when the priests pour out offerings of water. Again, the prophet's words run through your head, "Living waters will flow

from Jerusalem...".[22]

You thought your famous brother had decided to let you celebrate in peace, but you were wrong. About half way through the week, you enter the temple with your family and see your brother, Jesus, teaching in the courts. The Pharisees send officers to arrest your troublesome sibling, but Jesus tells them there is no need. He is leaving; he is going to a place where they cannot go.

The last day, the great day of the feast, has finally arrived. The priests have their jars filled with water and will pour them out on the altar at the temple.[23] How

---

[22] Zechariah 14:6-8
[23] Kasdan, "God's Appointed Times", p. 98.

you have longed for this day along with all the others in attendance. At the pouring, the crowds erupt with joy. They dance, sing, shout and clap in happy celebration as they recite the Hallel Psalms.[24] The waters of life have been poured out as the towers of light shine brightly.

Then you hear your oldest brother cry out amongst the joyous throng, "If anyone thirsts, let him come to me and drink. He who believes in me, just as the scriptures say, out of his belly will flow rivers of living water!" Again, he makes another embarrassing announcement: "I am the light of the world. The ones who follow me will not walk in darkness, but have the light of life."

---

[24] Psalms 113-118

Your heart sinks. Jesus, your brother, has seemingly gone mad. It was bad enough when he spoke of "eating his flesh" and "drinking his blood", but this has gone too far. He is claiming to be the conclusion and fulfillment of one of the greatest feasts you have ever known or celebrated. This feast has always been celebrated in, not only remembrance of what God had done with the tabernacle of Moses, anticipation of what God would one day do.

Zechariah told of a time when there would be no sun or stars, only light by day and night. All the nations of the earth would come and celebrate as one this "Day of Holiness" unto the Lord. Jesus claimed to be that fulfillment. In him and him alone will one find living water.[25] Only in him will the nations have the light of life within them.

James, one of the brothers of Jesus who had ridiculed him in John 7 and was most certainly ashamed of his brother's statements during this feast, came to believe those statements as true. After Jesus rose from the dead, James came to see that his brother was not at all crazy or delusional. Instead, He was what God had been planning all along. When God told His firstborn son, Israel, to celebrate this feast, He had His only begotten son in mind. James came to realize this. He "ate His flesh" and "drank His blood", and therefore had the Light of Life in him; he

---

[25] See John 4:10

had the River of Living Water flowing from him. James now knew that his brother was indeed the fulfillment of the Feast of Tabernacles.

It isn't any wonder that John began his gospel by referring to Jesus as God in flesh: the God who "tabernacled" with us and we beheld His glory. He speaks of Him being the light of life that gives light to every man. He turns water in jars into the best wine. He gives a living water where we can drink and never thirst again, a water that springs up to life eternal.

For millennia, God had ordained this feast in honor of His son who would come, die and rise to new life. We can come to Him and celebrate the light and the living water.

As with so many feasts, this one too looks forward prophetically to a time yet to come. In Revelation 21 and 22, because the slaughtered Lamb of God has risen from the dead, victorious over the nations, there is a time coming when the creation itself will be renewed to its full glory. God will one day fully tabernacle with His people and there will be no need for a temple any longer. There will be no sun or moon, for the glory of God will radiate and illuminate this renewed creation. God will rule from His throne and the River of Life will flow from the place where He reigns supreme. This is the ultimate destination of the Feast of Tabernacles. Let the church wait faithfully for the day, and may we eagerly await its coming. Amen.

Scriptures and Occasion of Feast

Leviticus 23:33-44

- 15th day of 7th month, 7-day feast
- High Sabbath
- Offerings given every day of celebration with special meetings on first and last day
- People of Israel would live in little booths made especially for this occasion to remember that they lived in booths as they left Egypt
- Booths traditionally made with 3 sides and a top that gave visibility to the sky above

Zechariah 14

- After the time of judgement, all the remnant of nations shall celebrate this feast
- Celebrates a time when there is no night and living waters roll from Jerusalem

John 7 & 8

- Jesus at feast claims to be the True Feast of Booths: He is Light, He gives Living Water

Revelation 21 & 22

- The new creation will be a feast of booths where there is no night and all who thirst can drink of the water of life

Chapter Nine

The Final Sabbath

Leviticus 23:3

Six days shall work be done, but on the seventh day is a Sabbath of solemn rest, a holy time. You will not do any work on this day; it is the Sabbath of the Lord in all your tents.

This was the first time you had ever met him. Until today, you had only heard stories about this man who seems to have entered onto the scene in a whirlwind. You heard of how he had spoken on the mountain to the masses and of how he had taught the people how to pray. You heard of his talk about not worrying, but having faith in the God who provides what is needed, even to the smallest of creatures.

Others said very little of his teachings, but spoke of his mighty acts. "I heard he healed a man with leprosy!" Others said excitedly, "I saw him heal a man who was paralyzed!" Still another announced, "I saw him raise a little girl from the dead."

The stories of his teaching and power were encouraging, but until today, these were only stories: stories of things that this man of God was doing for everyone else but you. They had found rest from their sorrows and trouble. They had been given peace and comfort for their sickness and disease, but you have yet to find rest for your weary soul. "If only he would come this way," you think to yourself. "Then, he could come and give me respite from my burdens."

Today turns out to be the day. This man, Jesus, and his disciples, have come to your town. And he is giving the speech you have been longing to hear for more years than you care to recall. "Come to me, all you who are weary and heavily burdened, and I will give you rest." His words roll over you like a warm blanket on a cold morning, just as the sun begins to rise. This is what you have been longing for! Would today be the day?

As you take your place at the local synagogue, your thoughts of peace and rest are interrupted. You hear the leaders of your beloved city and place of worship murmuring about how this Jesus was a law breaker. "He dared to harvest grains on the Sabbath. He knows nothing about the Sabbath or the law." As they speak to one another, their glances in your direction do not go unnoticed. In extreme discomfort, you sit and wait to see what might happen. You slowly slip your withered hand inside your garments as their glances turn to blatant staring.

In that moment, Jesus, the Sabbath-working law-breaker, enters the building. Before a single word had been spoken, your leaders and teachers since youth stand up, glaring at Jesus indignantly. One of them, with a wry grin, asks Jesus accusingly, "Is it lawful to heal on this day of rest?" You look up and notice that the entire group is fixated on you. You dare not take your hand out of your robe, but you know that it doesn't matter. Everyone knows it is you they are talking about. You are the one who needs healing.

You then remember that Jesus had already answered this question earlier that day, in the field where they were eating.

"Didn't David, when the need was great, break the Sabbath and God blessed it? Do not the priests work blamelessly on the Sabbath?" You had never thought of this, but the answer is obvious.

Now, in the synagogue, Jesus turns the tables and asks them a question: "Do you not break the Sabbath, if a sheep falls in a pit? Do you not pull it out?" The answer, again, is obvious. "Of course they do," you think to yourself. Part of you wonders how you had never seen this before.

Jesus, knowing that they unwillingly agree with him, then makes yet another obvious statement. "Therefore, it is lawful to do good on the Sabbath."

Now, his gaze turns to you. "Stretch out your hand," he says. You slowly remove your hand from its hiding place and reach out in his direction. You feel the strength, strength you haven't felt in that hand since childhood, return. You begin moving your fingers and opening and closing your hand rapidly. You look to the leaders who have known you since your childhood days, but you soon wish you could hide your joy as well as you had hidden your hand. But you cannot quench the excitement. They could not quench their hatred. No one likes to be proven wrong, especially when they know they are right. Jesus truly is "Lord even of the Sabbath."

You, for one, had finally found rest. His words may have led others to wrath and plots of destruction, but for you, his words were nothing but pure, real, true and complete Sabbath.

Every Saturday, the Jews would take a break from their labors and work. They would remember that even God rested from His work of creation on the seventh day. It was a holy time of rest.

Jesus did not come to nullify the Sabbath, the day of rest. He came to fulfill it. Throughout the gospels, Jesus, time and time again, does good on the day of holy rest. He heals the sick and makes people who had no rest from their broken bodies to finally find rest. He tells them that the

Sabbath was made for man, not the other way around. He is Lord over this day!

Every Sabbath, in this way, was meant to be a day when the people of God could rest from their work and trouble. They were to take a break from their toils and rest in the grace and provision of God. Yes, they were even called to remember the time, before the fall of man, when God Himself rested in His newly created temple: creation itself. Remembering this time should cause them (and us) to also look forward to the time when the true Sabbath would come and creation would be restored, renewed and made whole.

When Jesus came, he came announcing that the long-awaited time had finally come. If the people of God would but go to him, he would in turn give them Sabbath. He would make them whole. He would give them true rest.

Sabbath was, by far, the most celebrated day of all as it was done every week. Every week, the nation of Israel would stop their work and celebrate Jesus, the true Sabbath for all creation. Yes, they certainly did not know it was Him they celebrated, but it was Him all the same. Only he can give true rest. May we find our rest in Him.

Scriptures and Occasion of Feast

Leviticus 23:3

- Celebrated every week on the Sabbath (7th day)
- All were to cease from their labors and in so doing, keep it holy (set apart unto the LORD)

Exodus 31:16-17

- Done to remember how God rested from His work of creation
- Just as God was refreshed from His labor, so too shall man be

John 5 & specifically verse 17

- Jesus states that His Father (God) has been working until now (working every Sabbath) and that He too must work

- *Jesus shows that true Sabbath is found when creation is put right and diseases are healed (Jesus healed a great many on the Sabbath, making this point clear)*

  Hebrews 3 & 4

- *God has always promised a true rest. Unbelief kept many out, but the people of God shall enter into His true rest*

  Revelation 14:13

- *Those who remain faithful and true shall inherit an eternal Sabbath*

Conclusion

John 5:46

For if you believed Moses, you would believe in Me, for he wrote about me.

Conclusion

The years of your life are now coming to a close. As you sit in a lonely prison cell, you sense that this is the end. In your loneliness, you pen these words: "For I am already being poured out as a drink offering, it is time for me to go. I have fought the good fight, finished the course. I have kept the faith. There is laid up for me a crown of righteousness that the Lord, the righteous judge, will give me on that Day. Not only to me, but to all who have loved His appearing."

In your heart, you know that these may be the last words you ever write to your beloved son in the faith, Timothy. And now, at the end of your days, you look back over the journey of your faith and how God has made such a major difference in your life through His own beloved son, Jesus.

In your mind, you travel back to the day that changed your life forever. You were on your way to a town called Damascus. If it hadn't been for what happened to you, no one would ever even know that this little place existed. You were a man on a mission to punish, persecute and even kill the followers of Jesus. Having heard that there were those in this town who were followers, you made it your personal duty to seek them out and throw them in prison. As far as you knew, it was your call from God to do this work.

Then it happened. An event that would change you completely and forever. With thoughts of imprisonment in your head and the blood of Stephen still on your hands, you meet Jesus. You hear his voice ask you, "Why are you persecuting Me, Saul?" The brightness of His glory was so brilliant that you actually fell from your horse, blinded by His splendor. "Why are you fighting against Me?" you hear Him ask.

Within a few short days, your entire life is turned upside down. For the first time, you can truly see as the scales of blindness fall from your eyes. The message of Jesus, the very message you did not understand and therefore chastised, was now your message. Everything is different now. You were blind to the message before, but now, through the Spirit of God, you can at long last see and understand.

You are just like Cleopas and his companion as they walked the weary road to another obscure town called Emmaus. Like them, you too were living with eyes that had been restrained. And, like them, you met Jesus on the road; this encounter with the savior changed everything.

In your cell, you recall all the years you spent celebrating the various festivals. You remember the joy of the Festival of Booths. You look fondly upon all the times you celebrated the Passover with your brothers. You remember the Feast of Trumpets, the Early Fruits and the Latter Fruits, The Day of Atonement and the Sabbath. In all your other writings, from Romans to even the one you write now, you show how Jesus was the fulfillment of them all.

Now, you, Paul the apostle, look back one final time and remember that in the Messiah, there is still one more appointed time to look forward to. You remind Timothy of this day, this new Day of Atonement, when Jesus appears and rewards His faithful followers.

It is because of Jesus that your faith makes sense. It is because of Jesus that the festivals of generations past and present have meaning. It is because of Him that every celebration ever performed has completion and fulfillment. You are able to die in hope. Your life and faith are not in vain. Thanks to Jesus, Messiah, High Priest, Lamb of God, your Passover, the Firstfruits, you have hope. Because of Him, you have a true Sabbath; rest from your toils. It is all about Him. It always has been, and so shall it ever more be.

Returning to our image from Martin Luther, through this book we have been slowly unwrapping the baby Jesus as He lies in a manger, swaddled in the cloths of the Old Testament celebrations. There, inside the cloths, we have found the Christ. He is beautiful. He is wonderful. He is able to open our eyes so we can understand Moses, believe him and thereby believe and know Jesus.

Additional Resources

Kasdan, Barney *God's Appointed Times*
1993 Messianic Jewish Publishers

Burge, Gary *Jesus and the Jewish Festivals*
2012, Zondervan

Sanders, E.P. *Judaism Practice and Belief*
2016 Fortress Press

Bock, Darrell L. *Who Is Jesus: Linking the Historical Jesus with the Christ of Faith*
(chapter 5, Jesus and the Sabbath)
2012 Howard Books

Made in the USA
Middletown, DE
29 October 2018